Exploring the Nature with a Map and Compass

www.sisuidrottsbocker.se

SISU Sport Books

Address:
SISU Idrottsböcker,
Idrottens Hus, SE-123 87 Farsta
Tel 08-605 60 00, fax 08-605 62 26
Orders:
SILVA Sweden AB
Kuskvägen 4, SE-191 62 Sollentuna
Phone: +46 8 623 43 00 Fax: +46 8 92 76 01
E-mail: info@silva.se Web:www.silva.se

© SISU Sport Books/SILVA
Text: Lasse Hogedal
Maps: Bertil Lundkvist
Layout: Ia Johannesson
Illustrations: Ingela Jondell
Photos: Aerial photo page 10 – Metria
(approved for publication 98-03-11)
Sjöberg Classic, page 4–5, 6, 46, 59 and cover
Keith Samuelson, page 54, 72, 77
PhotoDisc™, page 29, 30, 45, 52–53, 60, 78, 84–85 and cover
Original: Sista Ordet AB
Printed by: Danagård Grafiska, Ödeshög, Sweden 1999
ISBN: 91-88940-46-2

Contents

Open Sesame!

The countryside is wonderful. Coast or inland, mountain or forest, heath or sand dunes, pine-forest or leafy wood – each has its own charm and attracts its own following.

The countryside is full of treasures. Birds and animals, mosses, flowers, trees and plants in millions of colours. Roaring waters, calm waters, running waters. Mountains that offer fantastic views. Magical lakes and snow, by no means just for the photographer. Peace, the sighing of the wind, pattering rain and warm sun offer their own dimensions.

For many of us, the countryside is a source of refreshment, leisure and recreation. The key to nature is a map and a compass. These tools open the door to new landscapes for exploration, for navigating waters with rocks and shoals, new fishing areas, game-shooting, not to mention the colourful and adventurous sport of orienteering!

A map is like Ali Baba's "Sesame" – it opens the door to the countryside. The compass is a simple but remarkable instrument that reassures and shows the way. This book will teach you how to use a map and compass.

Welcome to the great outdoors!

1. The map
– a simplified view!

A simplified view

A map is a simplified view of the surface of the earth seen from above and greatly reduced in size. Exactly how much the map is reduced in size is apparent from the scale that is always given on a map.

In our daily lives we come across all sorts of maps. They vary in colour, signs and symbols. However, they are all based on the same idea – to give a simplified view of the earth's surface seen from above and reduced in size. Two types of maps are illustrated below:

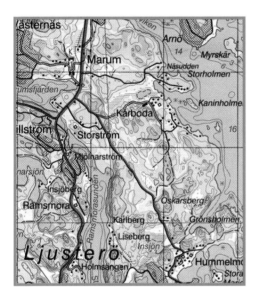

"Gröna kartan"   **"Fjällkartan"**

The "Gröna kartan" and the "Fjällkartan" are examples of Swedish topographical maps – a type of map common in most countries.

Maps vary in quality. Some are schematic and generalised while others are very exact and full of detail. Below are two maps of the same area but differing in scale. In the upper map the land-area shown has been reduced 50 000 times and the lower map by 10 000 times.

 Scale 1:50 000

Scale 1:10 000

Scale 1:10 000 means that the land has been reduced 10 000 times on the map. Everything is 10 000 times smaller.

Using a scale of 1:10 000, 1 mm on the map corresponds to 10 000 mm = 10 metres on the ground

1:10 0~~00~~

A simple rule of thumb: Take away the last three noughts of the scale, as in the example above, and then 1 millimetre on the map is translated into 10 metres on the ground.

Far less detail can be shown on a map at a scale of 1:50 000 than one at 1:10 000.

The following table shows how many metres on the ground, each millimetre on the map corresponds to using different scales. For example, 50 mm on a map to scale 1:1 000 represents 50 metres in reality while on a scale of 1:20 000, 80 mm would represent 1 600 metres.

Scale	Millimetres									
	10 mm	20 mm	30 mm	40 mm	50 mm	60 mm	70 mm	80 mm	90 mm	100 mm
1:1 000	10 metres	20 metres	30 metres	40 metres	50 metres	60 metres	70 metres	80 metres	90 metres	100 metres
1:5 000	50 metres	100 metres	150 metres	200 metres	250 metres	300 metres	350 metres	400 metres	450 metres	500 metres
1:10 000	100 metres	200 metres	300 metres	400 metres	500 metres	600 metres	700 metres	800 metres	900 metres	1 000 metres
1:15 000	150 metres	300 metres	450 metres	600 metres	750 metres	900 metres	1 050 metres	1 200 metres	1 350 metres	1 500 metres
1:20 000	200 metres	400 metres	600 metres	800 metres	1 000 metres	1 200 metres	1 400 metres	1 600 metres	1 800 metres	2 000 metres
1:25 000	250 metres	500 metres	750 metres	1 000 metres	1 250 metres	1 500 metres	1 750 metres	2 000 metres	2 250 metres	2 500 metres
1:50 000	500 metres	1 000 metres	1 500 metres	2 000 metres	2 500 metres	3 000 metres	3 500 metres	4 000 metres	4 500 metres	5 000 metres
1:100 000	1 000 metres	2 000 metres	3 000 metres	4 000 metres	5 000 metres	6 000 metres	7 000 metres	8 000 metres	9 000 metres	10 000 metres
1:250 000	2 500 metres	5 000 metres	7 500 metres	10 000 metres	12 500 metres	15 000 metres	17 500 metres	20 000 metres	22 500 metres	25 000 metres

A. If you measure 1 mm on a map to a scale of 1:5 000 how many metres is that on the ground?

B. If you measure 5 mm on a map to a scale of 1:10 000 how many metres is that?

C. If you measure 10 mm on a map to a scale of 1:20 000 how many metres is that?

D. If you measure 3 mm on a map to a scale of 1:5 000 how many metres is that?

E. If you measure 20 mm on a map to a scale of 1:100 000 how many metres is that?

The language of the map

In order to make the map easy to read and readily comprehensible, various colours and symbols are used. It is not possible to indicate all of the features and objects; otherwise the map would contain too many features and be difficult to read. The symbols used on a map represent as closely

as possible, the features on the ground. The picture on the left is an aerial view of an area. Water, roads, fields and buildings can be identified after some study. There is also a map of the same area below it. This gives a very much clearer picture of the same area.

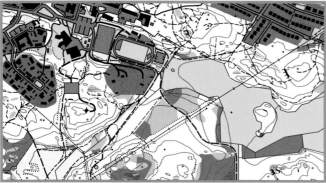

As we have noted earlier, there are many different types of maps at various scales and using different colours and symbols. There are maps for all sorts of uses from leisure activities to specialised maps for the military, for meteorologists, surveyors or geologists. A good rule for looking at a new map is to first look at the legend, which explains the symbols and indicates the scale. In this book we use a map specially drawn for orienteering and outdoor activities.

Map symbols enable anyone, regardless of which country they come from, to read all maps. One advantage of the orienteering map is that the symbols, colours, scales and the thickness of the lines etc., are to a world standard. They are determined by the International Orienteering Federation (IOF) which is the reason why IOF orienteering maps are used in this book

Another advantage is that they are normally at scales of 1:10 000 and 1:15 000. This means a lot more very helpful detail can be shown to anyone navigating on foot. The most common map scale produced by national cartographic organisations for walkers, is about 1:25 000. A good source for information about maps for your area is your local library.

The following colours apply to orienteering maps. Six or seven colours are normally used .

- *The WHITE areas denote runable forest*
- *Anything BROWN has to do with differences of altitude: mountains, heights, ravines and hollows.*
- *Everything YELLOW represents open land: fields, meadows or forest clearings.*
- *GREEN indicates dense, impenetrable forest; the darker the colour the more impenetrable it is.*
- *YELLOW/GREEN indicates land that is built on, for example gardens and lawns.*
- *BLUE areas and features are to do with water.*
- *BLACK is the most colour used and indicates numerous things such as roads, paths, power-lines, buildings, rocks and precipices.*

For standard topographic maps, white normally means open areas and green means wooded areas.

Symbols

Symbols on the map are drawn in different colours. Below is a list of the most common symbols and their colours.

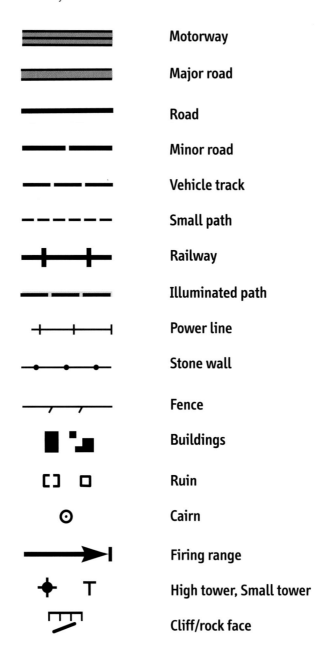

	Motorway
	Major road
	Road
	Minor road
	Vehicle track
	Small path
	Railway
	Illuminated path
	Power line
	Stone wall
	Fence
	Buildings
	Ruin
	Cairn
	Firing range
	High tower, Small tower
	Cliff/rock face

• ⚶	Boulder, boulder field
	Contour lines
∨	Pit
∪	Small depression
• ᵕ	Spot height
⬤	Lake/open water
	Uncrossable marsh
	Marsh, open marsh
	Indistinct marsh
	Crossable small watercourse
	Crossable watercourse
	Minor water-channel
••••••••••••	Narrow marsh
○	Well
ᴗ	Spring
∨	Waterhole
	Asphalt/paved area
	Open land
	Dense vegetation, the darker the green the more dense
	Settlement

TEST YOURSELF (Answers are at the back of the book)

• In the left column you will find a number of map symbols marked with a ring. Which of the drawings to the right corresponds with the respective symbol. The red and white, square symbol indicates the object.

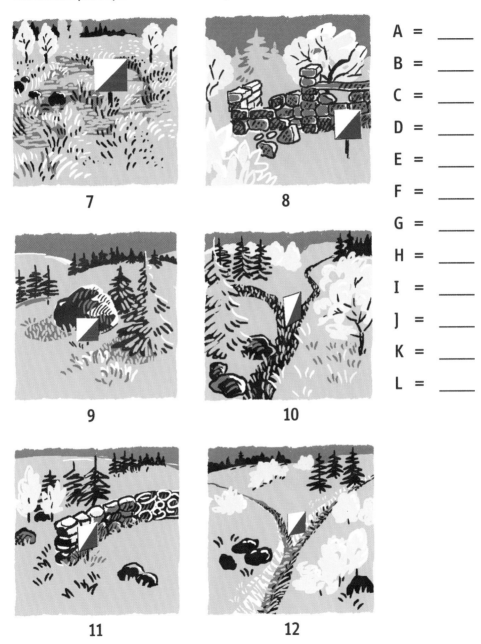

A = _____

B = _____

C = _____

D = _____

E = _____

F = _____

G = _____

H = _____

I = _____

J = _____

K = _____

L = _____

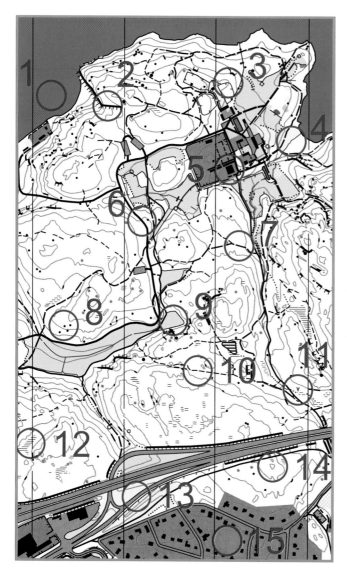

• On the map below 15 features are circled and numbered in red. The feature to be identified is in the middle of the circle. What is the meaning of the colour and symbol of each feature?

• In the previous test the scale was 1:10 000. What is the distance on the ground, between the following points (measured between the centres of the circles):

A. 3-4
B. 8-12
C. 10-15
D. 1-5
E. 7-14

Contour lines

Contour lines give very interesting information about differences in height. They also indicate where there are precipices, valleys and peaks as well as how steep the terrain is.

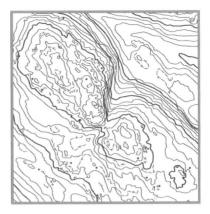

Cut out

It is now time to cut and glue your own little peak. It will help with the explanations to come. Extract the loose sheet marked "Make a peak" and follow the instructions at the bottom of the page.

A model

You now have a simple model of a hill (a peak) in front of you. Compare it with the map below. This is how height is indicated on the map.

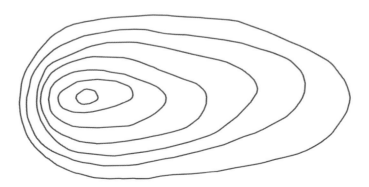

The difference in height between the contours on an orienteering map is normally five metres. But just as the scale can differ between different maps the equidistance (interval) between contours also differs. The key, or legend, to the map usually indicates the height between the contour lines.

The more contours there are, the higher the hill. Note too, that when the contours are close together, the ground is steep and when there are few contours, the slope is gentle.

A hill is not always as smooth and regular as on the model. Often the slopes are pitted with crevices and ravines. There may also be several knolls on the same area of high ground.

Some examples:

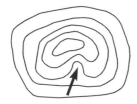

If one or more contours goes "inwards", this indicates a hollow, that is a ravine, re-entrant or gully.

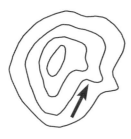

If one or more contours goes "outwards", this shows a spur or ledge that sticks out.

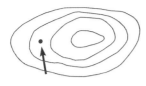

A brown dot shows a little hill (or knoll), the size of which does not affect the contour above it, or the one below it. It may be only 1–2 metres high.

A brown contour with "ticks" indicates a gravel pit.

A brown "v" or "u" means a small pit (1–2 metres in diameter).

Contours that meet and are shown with short lines (ticks) pointing inwards mean a hollow/depression, or a deeper pit.

TEST YOURSELF (Answers are at the back of the book)

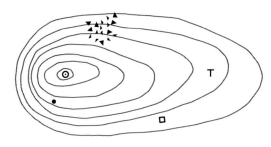

• On the hill to the left there are five different map symbols. What do the signs mean and where should they be placed on the model you have built?

• Clarify using the map below:

– How many knolls are there?

– Are there any knolls of equal height?

– Where is it steep?

– Which is the biggest re-entrant?

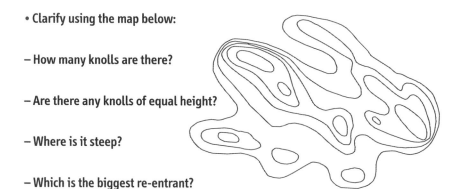

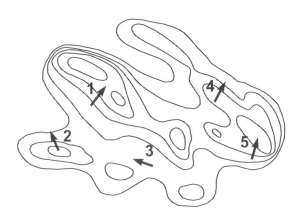

• Some arrows have been drawn on the map and given numbers. State whether the terrain goes upwards, downwards or is flat in the direction the arrows are pointing.

• Below there are eight peaks seen from the side. Which map belongs to which peak?

1. _____

2. _____

3. _____

4. _____

5. _____

6. _____

7. _____

8. _____

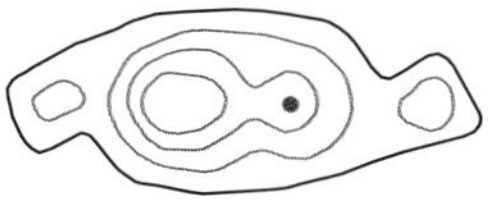

A

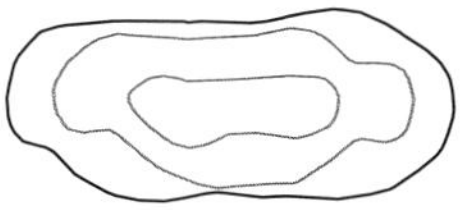

B

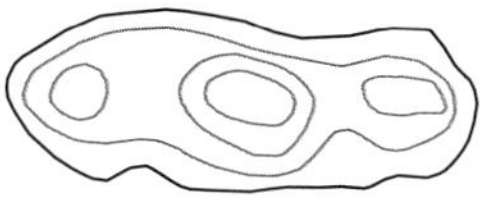

C

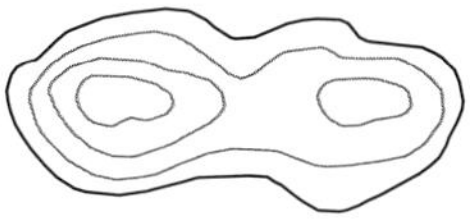

D

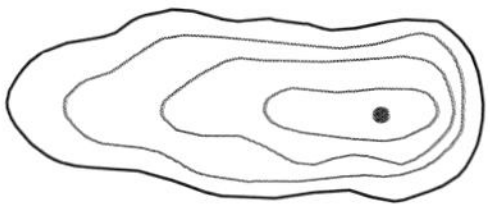

E

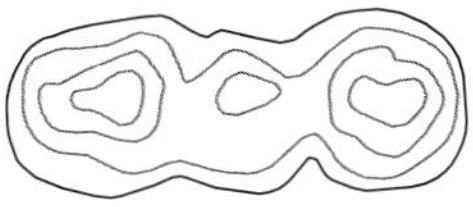

F

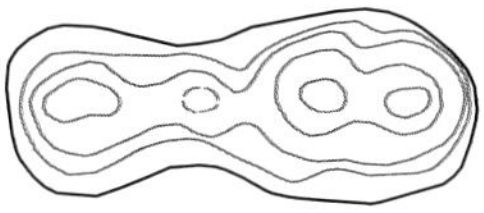

G

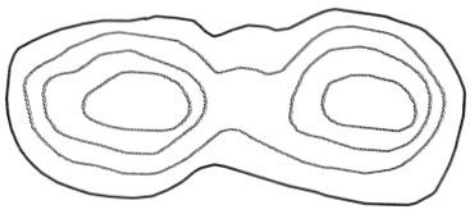

H

• In the left column you will find a number of map symbols in circles. Which of the sketches on the right goes with which symbol? The little red and white square symbol indicates the feature.

 A = ____

 B = ____

 C = ____

 D = ____

 E = ____

 F = ____

 G = ____

 H = ____

 I = ____

 J = ____

1

2

3

23

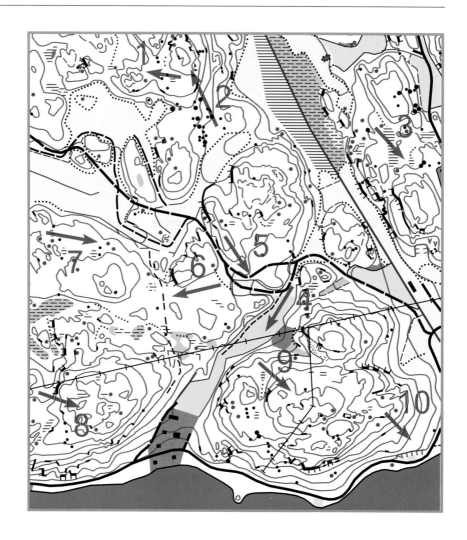

• On the map above there are 10 numbered, red arrows. State whether the terrain slopes upwards or downwards or is flat in the direction the arrow is pointing.

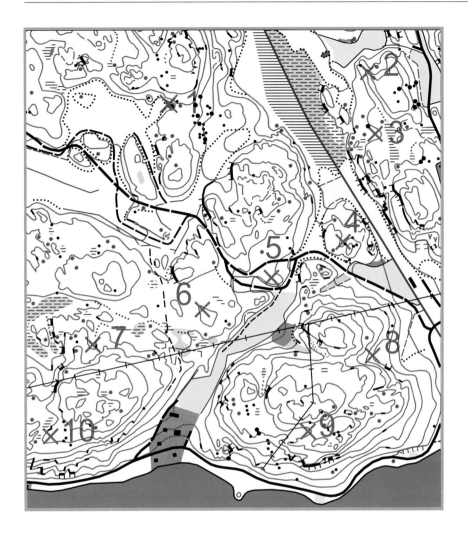

• On the map above there are 10 small, numbered "x-'s". State whether the "x" is placed in a re-entrant or a ridge.

How to use the map

You now understand how a map is organised using different colours and symbols. To use the map, in other words to read it, requires one essential action: the map has to be orientated.

The map can be compared with a piece in a jigsaw puzzle. The piece can only be fitted into the puzzle in one way. The same is true of maps. They only fit the terrain in one way. When north is at the top of the map, which it usually is, south is at the bottom, west to the left and east to the right.

In the example to the left, the map has been orientated to the terrain. Features to the right – the lake, for example – are on the right of the map. The shop, the school and the sports field which are to the left of the road are also on the left of the map.

TEST YOURSELF (Answers are at the back of the book)

• Below are four sketches of different areas. Beneath each sketch there are three map sections. Which map section is correctly orientated?

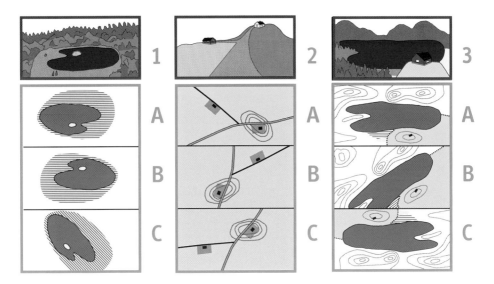

• Below there is a view of a landscape and a map of the same area. In the view you will find features marked with the letters A, B, C, D, E, F and G. The same features are shown on the map indicated by the usual map symbols. Draw rings round these.

It is usually easiest to orientate the map when you see large and conspicuous objects or features. These may be buildings, a road or a lake, for example. If you do not see any particularly prominent features you can orientate the map with the help of a compass. There is more about that in the next chapter.

- *At 6 a.m. the sun is in the east, at noon in the south and at 6 p.m. in the west.*

- *Normally, because of the sun's position, the heaviest branches grow on the south side of trees.*

- *Moss and lichen normally grow on the north side of trees where there is most moisture.*

- *Anthills, many of them found near trees or boulders, are normally built on the sunny side i.e. south side.*

- *A free standing anthill normally has its steepest side facing north.*

- *On a starry night, the North Star indicates north. It is situated directly above the Plough constellation. For centuries, the North Star has acted as the seafarer's compass.*

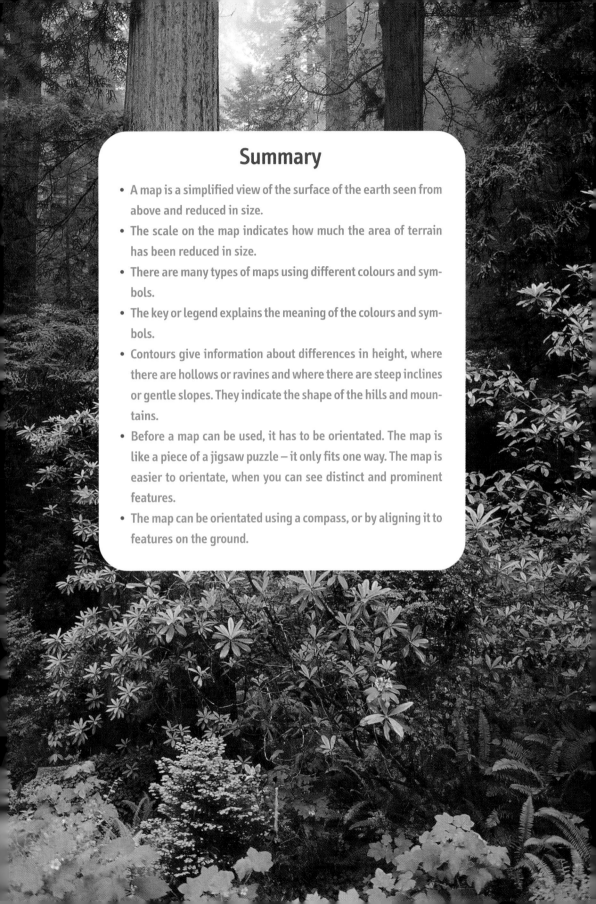

Summary

- A map is a simplified view of the surface of the earth seen from above and reduced in size.
- The scale on the map indicates how much the area of terrain has been reduced in size.
- There are many types of maps using different colours and symbols.
- The key or legend explains the meaning of the colours and symbols.
- Contours give information about differences in height, where there are hollows or ravines and where there are steep inclines or gentle slopes. They indicate the shape of the hills and mountains.
- Before a map can be used, it has to be orientated. The map is like a piece of a jigsaw puzzle – it only fits one way. The map is easier to orientate, when you can see distinct and prominent features.
- The map can be orientated using a compass, or by aligning it to features on the ground.

2. The compass

The magnetic compass

It is only necessary to use an eye-level or sighting compass (which can be a lensatic, mirror or prismatic compass), when great accuracy is essential. Orienteerers navigate at speed and with accuracy through thick forest and across featureless terrain in the dark or mist, using a Silva protractor compass.

Lensatic compasses have a means of viewing the rotating compass card, with the bearing scale printed on it. The scale is viewed through a magnifying lens, via a mirror set at 45°. The hairline is aligned from the reflected scale to *under* the object in the distance. Such instruments should be accurate to within 1°.

Prismatic compasses should be accurate to within 0.5°. The scale is viewed through a single prism and because of an optical illusion the hairline appears *over* the object, making it easy to take very accurate readings.

The accuracy of the compass is of course important, but because good quality protractor compasses are accurate to within 2 degrees, it is the ability of the navigator to use the compass accurately, that is far more important.

Other types of compasses are Braille, Prayer, Military (mils scale 6400 mils = 360°), escape and evasion, survival, car (including electronic for vehicles), boats and planes, diving, and of course, orienteering.

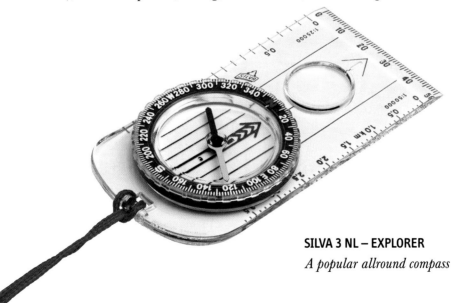

SILVA 3 NL – EXPLORER
A popular allround compass

With the help of a Silva protractor compass you can rapidly and easily get your bearings. There are many types of compass, which vary in appearance and which may be equipped with different types of scales. Here are some examples:

SILVA 40 SERE

Watch compass

A small survival compass that can be fitted to your watchstrap.

SILVA 19 LEARNER

Clip compass

Clip-on compass or road atlas page marker, is clipped to the map.

SILVA 1S EXPLORER

Protractor compass

This is a hand-held compass attached to the wrist by a cord.

SILVA 6 JET SPECTRA

Thumb compass

The thumb compass is fitted to the left or right thumb using a strap.

Always pointing north

All hand-held compasses have one thing in common – the magnetic needle or card! The coloured part, most often red, always points north, providing there are no objects made of iron (ferrous metal), magnets or other compasses in the immediate vicinity.

See what happens as you approach an iron object!

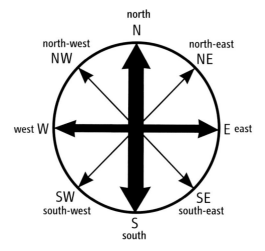

North, south, east and west are called the cardinal points. North-east, south-east etc. are called the inter-cardinal points.

Pointer to the magnetic pole

What is it that makes a compass needle consistently point in a north-south direction? The answer is the powerful but invisible force known as magnetism. The earth is like a giant magnet. Magnetism was discovered a very long time ago. People found that lodestones (stones containing magnetic oxide of iron) – placed on a piece of wood floating in a bowl of water, always turned and took up a fixed position. The compass had been invented!

It is a matter of argument who first had the idea of letting a lodestone show the north-south bearing. Scholars believe that the Chinese were the first to exploit the phenomenon. "Si Nan" is considered to have been the first compass. Si Nan means "the southern governor" and is symbolised by a ladle whose handle points south. Si Nan was part of a fortune-telling board consisting of two parts – one part symbolising the earth and the other symbolising heaven.

Since the ladle was rather imprecise, the Chinese started magnetising needles in order to gain greater precision and stability. According to Chinese writings, the first compasses were used at sea about the year 850. The invention was then spread by astronomers and mapmakers along the routes west to Indians, Muslims and Europeans.

The compass was developed over centuries and a major breakthrough came when it was discovered that a thin piece of metal could be magnetised, by stroking it with a lodestone.

The next stage involved enclosing the compass needle in an air-filled and transparent container, a so-called compass bowl. In this way the needle was protected.

Compasses of yesteryear suffered from the compass needle swinging wildly and taking a long time to stabilise. Modern compasses are precision instruments and the needle, which is now normally enclosed in a housing cavity filled with a liquid, rapidly settles to north-south.

Magnetic variation (declination)

Magnetic north, to which the needle points, is not exactly at the North Pole as defined by the meridians. Most maps show meridians, which are north-south lines. These pass through the geographical North Pole. Meridians are thin lines and usually printed black.

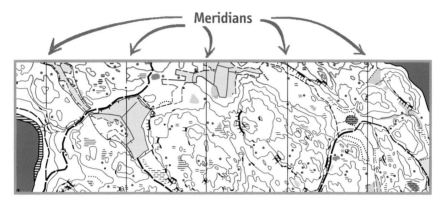

Variation arises because the magnetic and geographical north poles do not coincide. It *varies* in different parts of the world. In Canada it can be over 40 degrees, but in Scandinavia, it is negligible. Modern maps used for leisure activities and for orienteering are printed with the meridians corrected for magnetic variation and printed to magnetic north.

Deviation

The compass needle can be influenced by deposits of iron ore, high-voltage power lines, iron posts and fences. Any influence results in incorrect readings (called deviation), unless the external magnetic field happens to be exactly in line with the north–south orientation of the needle and of opposite polarity. The chances of that are remote.

Golden rules

1. Store and use your compass well away from any magnetic field
2. Check that your compass functions correctly before you leave home and in time to rectify any problems you may find

If you do not keep to the above rule, there is the very real danger of reversing the polarity of the needle. This applies to any make of compass, especially those with poor quality weak magnetic needles. The compass needle can be re-polarised. (See your compass dealer.)

Orientation with a compass

In the preceding chapter we noted that maps should always be orientated when navigating. The compass enables you to orientate maps, as magnetic north is always indicated on the map. North is normally at the top of the map. When the magnetic meridians are parallel with the compass needle the map is orientated. The north-seeking end of the needle, must be to the north end of the meridian.

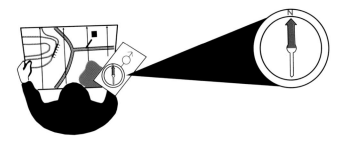

The Silva "clip-on-compass" (Model 19) can be fixed on to the map. The map is orientated when the north end of the compass needle, is parallel to and pointing to the north end of the magnetic meridians on the map.

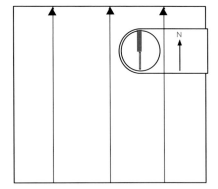

Your friend the compass

Your compass will help you to:

- *orientate the map*
- *move in particular directions*

It is easiest to follow a bearing due north, south, east and west. We shall look at other bearings later.

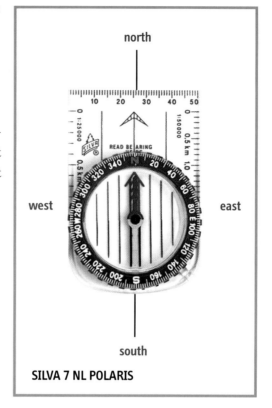

SILVA 7 NL POLARIS

TEST YOURSELF

• Use a compass to find out where north, south, east and west are in relation to your own position.

• If you have a map of where you are, orientate it using a compass.

TEST YOURSELF (Answers are at the back of the book)

• Which of the maps below is orientated with which compass?

1 ____

2 ____

A

B

3 ____   4 ____

C

D

Taking a bearing

When you want to move more accurately in a particular direction, you should use a compass. The Silva baseplate compass is carried with a cord around your wrist. Certain details of the compass should be noted especially:

1. *Arrow showing direction of travel*
2. *Index mark where the compass bearing is read*
3. *The compass needle*
4. *"N" on the compass housing*
5. *North-south lines on the bottom of the compass housing*

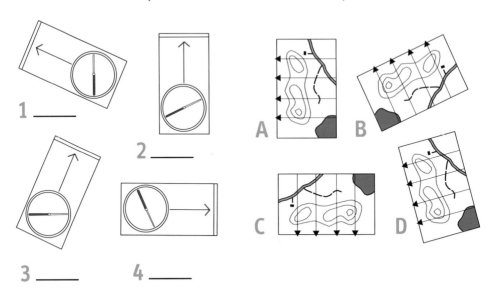

SILVA 1S EXPLORER

In addition, there are scales on the baseplate for measuring and the compass housing is graduated in 360 degrees.

The SILVA 1-2-3 System©

Follow the simple SILVA 1-2-3 System exactly and you will be armed with the navigation aid, which has probably guided more navigators on foot all over the world, than anything else in recent history.

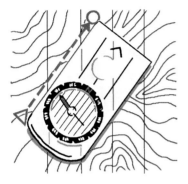

• Place the compass on the map with one edge in line with where you are and pointing in the direction of where you want to go.

• Turn the compass so that N on the housing points north on the map. You can also make use of the north-south lines in the bottom of the housing. These should be parallel with the meridians on the map with red lines pointing north and black lines pointing south.

• Remove the compass from the map and hold it horizontally in front of you. Turn your body so that the coloured (red) part of the needle is pointing to "N" on the compass housing.

• Now move in the direction that the "direction of travel" arrow shows on the baseplate.

It is a lot easier to accurately point a compass with a long baseplate. To illustrate the point, try showing directions to someone using a stick about one inch (a couple of centimeters) long with your arm bent and then use a long stick, with your arm extended. It is easier to point it in the right direction, if it is held in both hands. When you have found out in which direction you should be moving, look for a feature on the ground. This can be an individual tree or other well-defined feature. When you reach the feature, you look for another feature and continue in this way until you reach your destination.

Magnetic variation (or declination)

In certain areas of the world, Magnetic Variation (MV) must be taken into account. MV, is the difference in degrees, between true north and magnetic north. The north-south meridians on maps other than orienteering maps, are aligned with true north. As previously explained, the magnetic compass needle always points to magnetic north.

When the MV is west the difference must be ADDED when working from grid (meridian) to magnetic bearings and subtracted when the MV is east. The reverse applies when working from magnetic bearings to grid.

Annual change

The magnetic variation changes a little throughout the year, as the magnetic north pole changes its position very slightly throughout the year. The amount of change each year, is called the annual change, but for recently printed topographic maps the change can be ignored for practical navigation.

Dip

The earth's magnetic lines of force dip downwards towards the polar regions. They are approximately horizontal at the equator. Between the equator and the poles, the needles therefore dip and have to balanced in order to counteract the effect of the dip.

A common mistake is for the compass to be held too low and close to the waist. The problem then, is that the line of sight must be accurately raised through a comparatively long arc, in the direction of the bearing being taken. The answer is to hold the compass as high as possible and out ahead of you, while still being able to see that the needle is parallel to the orienting lines in the bottom of the capsule.

The thumb compass

The thumb compass is used on the left or right hand depending on the version and is fixed round the thumb with a strap. There are only two important details to be noted:

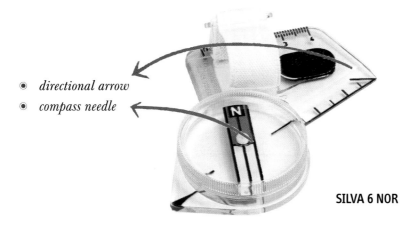

- *directional arrow*
- *compass needle*

SILVA 6 NOR

There are also measuring scales. The compass is normally held on the map all the time – the two forming a unit. Thumb compass housings are usually fixed although some models have a movable housing. The latter models can be used like a protractor compass.

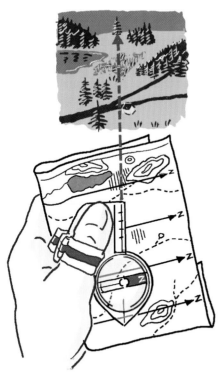

• Place the thumb compass with the directional arrow pointing from where you are to where you want to go.

• Hold the compass and map as a unit, horizontally in front of you. Turn your body so that north on the compass needle is pointing to magnetic north on the map.

• Move in the direction that the arrow shows, noting features in the terrain.

TEST YOURSELF (Answers are at the back of the book)

• In the sketch shown to the right, ten different bearings are shown. The starting point is shown by a triangle at the centre. Using a protractor compass take bearings from the middle of the triangle to the middle of the respective circles. For each bearing that you take, read off the number of degrees on the compass at the index mark.

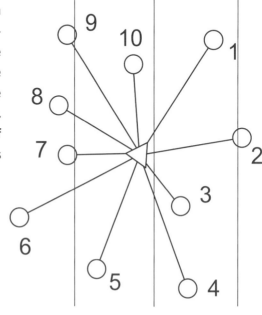

42

Sometimes things go wrong

In a hurry one can make a mistake when taking a bearing. A common error is placing the "N" of the compass to the south instead of the north on the map. You then move in exactly the opposite direction to the one intended.

Another common error is not looking at the compass often enough when you have decided on your direction. There is then a risk that you travel to the left or the right of your intended direction of travel, when following a compass bearing. This is because the compass is not aimed correctly.

In an experiment, five people were to move 500 metres in a given direction without a compass. At the start (marked with a triangle on the figure below) they were able to get their bearings from a compass that had been set. After that they were to follow the bearing as carefully as possible without a compass. The results of their movements are shown in the figure.

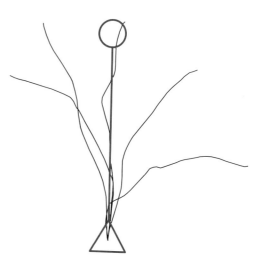

As can be seen there were large devia-tions from the original bearing. From this we can conclude that we suffer from an obvious inability to maintain a direction without navigational aids. The tendency to travel to the left or the right explains why people travel in circles and find them-selves back at the place they started from. You should continuously check your bear-ings with the help of a compass.

TEST YOURSELF

• Find a large open space. Decide on a point you wish to move to. Cover your eyes and try to go in the right direction. Uncover your eyes after a while and see where you end up.

An old method

An old method of keeping roughly to a bearing in dense forest without a compass is to use a pole or stick about 3–5 metres long. This acts as a "rudder" and lessens the risk of walking in circles.

In order not to lose your bearing when passing through thick bushes or similar obstacles, you push the stick through the bushes. You then move around the obstacle and move in the direction of the stick.

Experience shows that it is easy to lose your bearings when obstacles appear in the terrain. These may be thick bushes, marshy areas or rocky terrain. It is important to correct your bearings and to return to the original direction if you are obliged to make a detour.

In passing a steep hill or slope there is a risk that you will unconsciously choose to go around the slope in order to avoid tiring and demanding climbs. You will soon end up going in the wrong direction.

Looking after your compass

- Keep it away from magnetic fields, iron, scissors, knives, radios, electrical circuits, cellular or mobile phones, etc.
- Petroleum-based products like insect repellant and cleaning agents may give the surface of the compass a milky look. It may also remove the markings (scales).
- Treat your compass like the measuring instrument that it is — take care of it and it will take care of you!

3. Other aids
to navigation

You can also make use of other ways of establishing direction.

The following examples apply to the northern hemisphere. In the southern hemisphere, read north for south and vice versa.

Your watch can be used as a compass

At six in the morning the sun is in the east, at twelve noon it is due south and at six in the evening it is in the west. If you can establish the direction of north (or any other cardinal point), you can estimate the direction to travel in for any bearing.

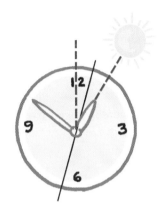

Using an analogue watch (one with a minute and hour hand), align the hour hand with the sun's direction. If you have a digital watch, draw a clock face showing the current time and align the drawing.

An imaginary line that bisects the angle between the hour hand (the suns direction) and 12 noon, is the north-south direction.

Note: The directions are reversed in the southern hemisphere.

- **Tree growth**
  Trees that stand alone usually have their biggest branches on the south side since that is where they get most sun.

- **Away from the heat of the sun**
  Moss and lichens grow mostly on the north side of trees and stones where it is dampest. *

- **Towards the heat of the sun**
  Anthills are often to be found by trees or rocks. They are most often built on the sunny, south-facing side*. An anthill usually slopes gently to the south and steeply to the north. This enables the ants to make maximum use of the sun for warmth. *

  *The opposite applies in the southern hemisphere

- **The stars**

  On a clear night the pole star is a good guide. It is to be found above the Great Bear and is always in the north. For many centuries the pole star has guided sailors. (Applies in the northern hemisphere only.) In the southern hemisphere the Southern Cross shows direction to the south.

GPS, SILVA Romer© and Protractor©-position

A grid reference refers to a unique position on any map. A location is indicated by an "easting" and a "northing" on a map, in the same way that longtitude and latitude indicate a position anywhere in the world.

There are well over 150 datums or grid systems, covering over 120 countries.

GPS

The Global Positioning System (GPS) is a satellite-based system that allows us to establish very rapidly exactly where we are anywhere in the world. To do this, an instrument that can receive signals from GPS satellites is needed. The GPS consists of about 24 satellites positioned about 20 000 kilometres above the earth in orbit in six different paths. Each satellite continuously emits a signal that can be picked up by GPS receivers on the ground.

The GPS receiver can measure the times taken for the satellite signals to reach the receiver. The speed of the signals is known (the speed of light is 300 000 kilometres per second), so the distances from the satellites can be calculated. If a signal is received from at least four satellites, the GPS receiver can calculate latitude, longitude and altitude (height above sea level).

GPS receivers are the size of an ordinary cellular phone. The receivers are relatively easy to use and in the future they will probably become an accepted navigation aid for people enjoying outdoor pursuits on land and water. Certain advanced GPS receivers can also show the route to a destination in the countryside. At sea, it is very helpful for information such as, speed, calculated time of arrival and drift from the intended direction to be shown.

The GPS receiver continuously updates its position and thus the current distance to and direction of the destination is shown. GPS now has many applications for navigation and for determining position.

The greatest benefit that GPS has brought to navigators on foot is, of course, the fixing of their position anywhere in the world. However, by fixing a position, it also establishes distance, something that no other instrument has ever been able to do.

Romer© and Protractor

The Romer divides a grid square into 100 squares (10 × 10 squares). Eastings divide the grid square into 10 columns east to west and the Northings into ten rows north to south.

If a map has a grid system, the system will almost certainly be explained in the margin of the map.

The Protractor is used to plot bearings accurately to and from the map or chart.

The SILVA combined Romer and Protractor is illustrated here.

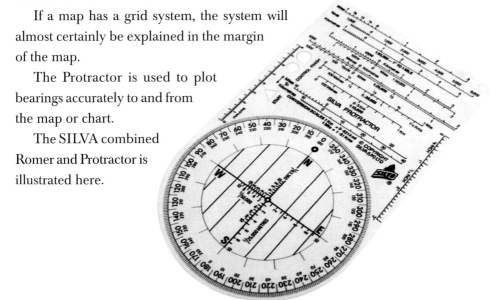

The SILVA Protractor

49

Height

⊙ **Altimeters**

The altimeter enables you to establish your height, to contour and to work out your rate of ascent/descent. The instrument becomes more important, the higher and more dangerous the mountains become.

Bearing in mind that the altimeter must be calibrated, in order to take into account the changing barometric pressure, you can usually expect an accuracy of about 5 metres.

Distance

⊙ **Pacing**

Pace counting is used by orienteerers to accurately estimate relatively short distances.

First, you need to establish how many paces you take per 100 metres. To do this, walk a known distance of 300 or 400 hundred metres on flat ground. Count the number of paces and find the average number taken per 100 metres. It is easier to keep count when pacing, if you count every time your left or right foot strikes the ground as one.

Next, produce a pacing scale, marking the divisions in tens of paces, according to the map scale you will use during the walk. In other words, measure the distance walked or to be walked, in numbers of paces, straight to and from the map.

Remember that your pace will shorten as you get tired, walk uphill, into the wind, over rough ground etc.

⊙ **Pedometers**

Without the use of a GPS instrument, distance is very difficult to measure over distances greater than about 500 or 600 metres. Up to that distance, pace counting, which is basically what a pedometer does, is more accurate. The pedometer saves you counting and converts the number of paces into a distance reading.

Any well-made pedometer is very accurate. However, the accuracy of the reading is dependent upon calibration and a consistent stride length.

Over longer distances, say over 500 to
600 metres, wind direction, the going
underfoot, height gain and/or loss and
your stamina, all effect your stride length
and therefore the distance displayed by the
pedometer.

Only experience will tell you when and
how much you can rely on a pedometer.
The more experienced you become, the less
you will need to use one.

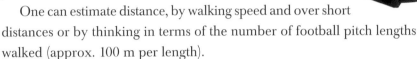

One can estimate distance, by walking speed and over short
distances or by thinking in terms of the number of football pitch lengths
walked (approx. 100 m per length).

On really steep mountains, an altimeter is sometimes more helpful.
The altimeter will tell you how many contour lines you have crossed and
therefore the distance on the map (the horizontal distance).

Again, experience counts a lot. It is important to get to know your
capability to cope with distances over different terrain. You may not even
know you true state of fitness, so test your fitness and your ability to
navigate, before going a long way into wild country.

Map measurers

The map measurer consists of a geared wheel, that is run along a route on
a map, connected to another gear attached to a needle.
The needle indicates on a scale, the distance measured.
An electronic measurer is now available,
which remembers a number of
scales and works with any
available map scale.

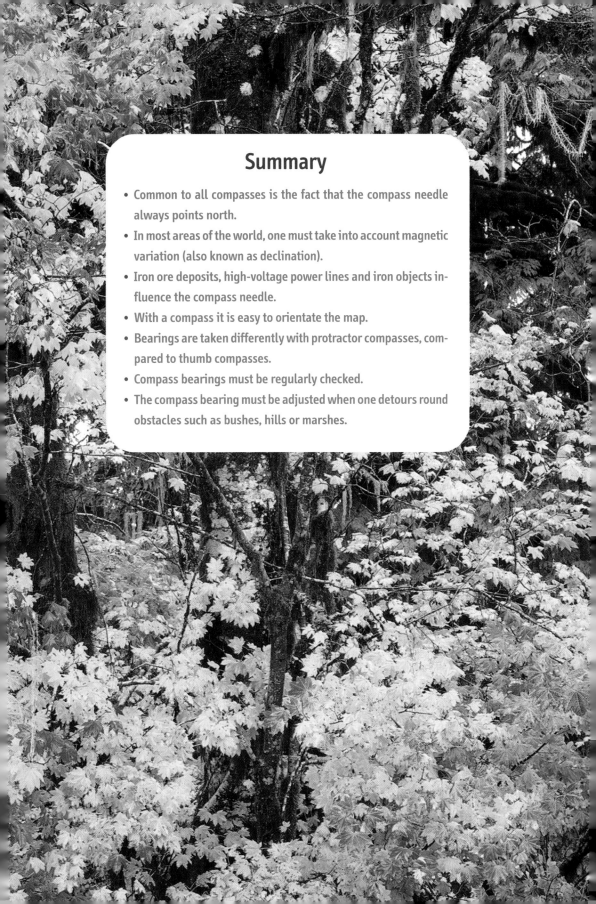

Summary

- Common to all compasses is the fact that the compass needle always points north.
- In most areas of the world, one must take into account magnetic variation (also known as declination).
- Iron ore deposits, high-voltage power lines and iron objects influence the compass needle.
- With a compass it is easy to orientate the map.
- Bearings are taken differently with protractor compasses, compared to thumb compasses.
- Compass bearings must be regularly checked.
- The compass bearing must be adjusted when one detours round obstacles such as bushes, hills or marshes.

4. Finding your way with a map and compass

Select a route

By route-selection we mean the route you decide to take before moving from one place to another. The routes we are interested in do not normally include roads or tracks even though you may perhaps follow a track along part of your route. There are often several possible routes between two places. The art of good route selection usually involves identifying the safest, (sometimes the quickest) and hopefully the least physically demanding route. However, during expeditions, advanced wild country training, elite competitions or other tests of extreme navigation, people may take calculated risks.

The most difficult terrain to navigate in is gently undulating, featureless moorland covering a very large area. With only a map and compass as aids to navigation, you must rely on "dead reckoning". This means using only direction and distance to find your way.

Good navigators nearly always know roughly where they are. In other words, they very rarely become completely lost.

We make many choices of route in our daily lives more or less subconsciously. Getting from home to school or to our place of work offers different possibilities. You can follow the road, take a short cut through a wood or choose a naturally pretty path. Your choice will depend on various factors: you may be in a great hurry, you may want a route that is smooth and flat or you may be looking for a pleasant experience and so choose a walk through the park.

Travelling by car, you can choose different types of roads. The fast motorway has its advantages, but you can also choose a gravel road that is shorter but takes longer to drive along and involves some navigation. You may prefer it because it runs through beautiful countryside.

You will reflect and make judgements in a similar manner on the basis of the information contained in the map when you move about in the forest, go hiking in the mountains or go across moorland. On each occasion you have to decide which route to take in order to fulfil your goal in the best way. The shortest route between two points is to go "straight there". But "straight there" is not always the most advantageous alternative. Consider the example in which "straight there" goes right over the

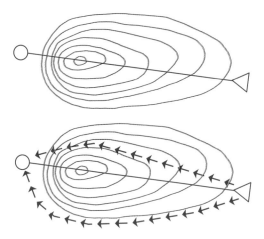

top of the hill. Compare, too, with the miniature peak that you can make from the loose sheet in this book. (See page 91.)

If you choose "straight there" you will have a difficult and tiring climb. Are there any alternatives? Yes, either you can choose a route to the left which is longer but which means that you do not have to climb the hill. Or you can take a route to the right. This route is also longer than "straight there" but does not involve so much climbing. You should consider various alternative before selecting your route.

Speed

When deciding on a fast route, it is not just a matter of avoiding high hills, you must also think about whether you can follow roads, paths, meadows or other types of terrain that will make your journey easier.

You move at different speeds in different types of terrain. The table that follows gives a rough indication of the time in minutes that it takes to move one kilometre in different types of terrain.

	Road	Meadow	Forest	Hilly wooded terrain
Walker	12	17	22	27
Jogger	6	8	10	14
Runner	4	6	8	10

This means, for example, that you gain by making a detour that is more than double the distance by road as compared with moving through hilly wooded country. The times given can, of course, vary. Passing through wet meadows early in the spring takes longer than when the meadow is dry and hard in the late summer.

Line features

When you select a route, it is always easiest to follow line features (sometimes referred to as handrail features). These can be roads, paths, power lines, edges of fields, stone walls, lake sides, streams and ditches.

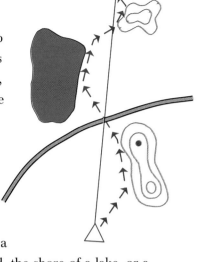

But there are not always line features that lead to your destination. So you then have to make use of other objects in the terrain and choose some distinct features that have to be passed. It is now that the compass really comes into its own. Examples of features are a definite and obvious rise, a road to be crossed, the shore of a lake, or a large hollow as in the example above. The starting point is marked with a triangle and the destination with a circle. The dotted line shows a possible route.

The compass shows the direction. Generally one should avoid following the compass over longer distances. As we noted in the preceding chapter, it is easy to go off course if you have to avoid a heap of rocks, a marsh or something similar. It is often difficult to correct such an error after passing the obstacle. For this reason one should always try to find a feature as close to the destination as possible.

TEST YOURSELF (Answers are at the back of the book)

- Which line features can you find on the map below? Mark their full length with a pen.
- Which line features are easiest to follow?

- Which conspicuous features can you find between the starting point (triangle) and the destination (circle) on the map below? Circle these.

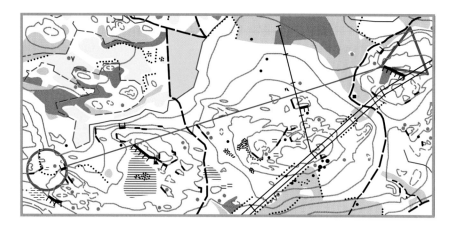

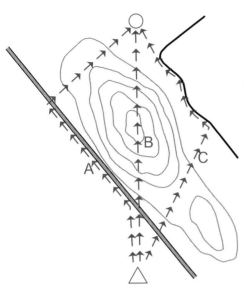

Which route to choose?

• In the example to the left, three different routes are marked. (The starting point is marked with a triangle and the destination with a circle.) Which one would you choose?

Some general points about choosing a route:

A: *A fast route, making use of the road, but somewhat uncertain. It is difficult to determine exactly where to leave the road. There is no definite attack point.*

B: *A difficult choice involving a long stretch using the compass and a steep hill to climb.*

C: *Perhaps the best alternative, which has a good attack point for the route, from the bend in the path, and means that you only need to follow the compass for a short distance.*

When you make use of different features, you have to be more careful about reading the map and using the compass than when following line features. The more experienced you become, the easier it becomes to judge the relative difficulty of different routes. You will soon learn to avoid steep hills or impenetrably marshy woods. On the map you will discover open rocks and paths that can be easily negotiated as well as impassable precipices and large areas of water.

TEST YOURSELF

• Below there are three sections of maps, each with a straight route marked. The designated starting point is marked with a triangle and the place you have to reach with a circle. Besides the "straight route" alternative, indicate two other possible routes for each journey.

• Explain the advantages and disadvantages of each route and indicate which is best.

• Explain which object in the terrain you would look out for when following your route.

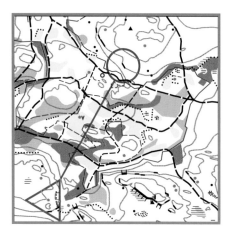

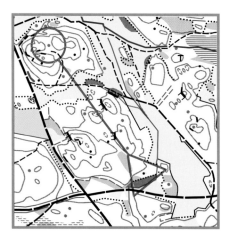

Safety first

If you have to move through featureless terrain without line features to a path-fork, you can naturally take a bearing with the compass and try to follow it as accurately as possible.

Aiming off

There is always a risk that you will have to move sideways to avoid bushes or suchlike and that you will then deviate from your bearing. When you finally reach the path you do not know whether the fork is to the left or the right.

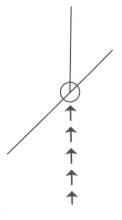

Instead, if you take a bearing to a point to the side of the fork (aim off), you will know which way to turn when you reach the path.

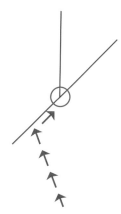

This will be the result!

You can use the same technique to reach the end of a lake. If you take a bearing to the end of the lake, there is a risk that you will aim off to the right and miss the lake.

Take instead a bearing to the left further down the lake. When you reach the lake you just aim off to the right and you are soon at the end of the lake.

This will be the result!

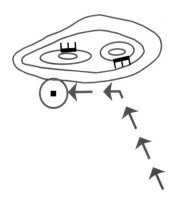

One further example is where you have to go to a hunting lodge at the foot of a large hill. You can take a bearing straight to the lodge but you risk walking to the left and missing the lodge. Instead, take a bearing to the right of the lodge. When the ground begins to rise steeply you merely have to aim off left to find the lodge.

Simplify

Try always to view the terrain in a larger perspective and not merely focus your vision on your destination. This is especially true if it is a small object.

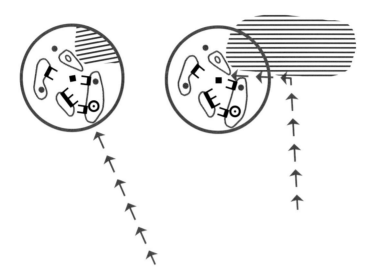

The hut may be difficult to find if you only look at the features in the immediate vicinity. Expand your view and discover the large marsh immediately beside it. Concentrate first on finding this and then the hut.

Follow the needle

You don't adjust the compass but instead move at a certain angle in relation to the compass needle.

In this example the starting point is marked with a triangle and the destination with a circle. You follow the red arrows by first going due south to the road and then following it as far as the bend before turning east.

Parallel error

This is a common map-reading error. You think that you are in a particular stretch of terrain or going along a line feature, when in fact you are on a different line that is parallel to the one you think you are on.

Often you do not discover the error immediately but in due course you end up in a different place than the one you intended. You can prevent the mistake by being extra careful when you are in an area with

many similar features, for example, numerous ravines or several hilly parts going in the same direction. Parallel error easily arises when using maps that have little detail or are of poor quality.

Taking a direct bearing

If you move towards a conspicuous feature, for example a hilltop, you can take a direct compass bearing on the feature. There may, of course, be a risk that it will not remain visible all the time – you may have to pass through a dense plantation for example.

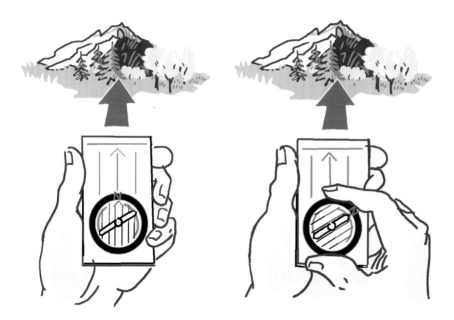

• The direction arrow on the compass is turned in the direction of the object.

• The compass is held horizontally in this direction while the compass housing is turned so that the "N" corresponds to the red, north end of the compass needle.

You now have your compass bearing and can proceed in the way described on page 39.

Cross-bearings

A method of using a compass to find out where you are. You have to be able to identify two objects or features that you can take back (reverse or back) bearings from. These might be at the end of a lake, a TV mast or a prominent building.

• Point the "direction-of-travel" arrow of the compass towards one of the feature.

• Hold the compass horizontally in this direction whilst turning the compass housing until the red, north end of the compass needle coincides with the "N" on the graduated ring on the housing.

• Place the compass on the map with either side of the baseplate touching the feature om the map. Rotate the compass (not the compass housing) untill the north/south orientating lines in the housing are parallel to the meridian lines on the map and ensure that the side of the baseplate is still on the feature. Draw a line along the edge of the baseplate.

• Select another object in the terrain and repeat the above three steps.

• Your position on the map should be where the two lines you have drawn intersect.

• A third feature can be selected and the same procedures followed for greater accuracy. The third line drawn on the map will in most cases result in a triangle called the "cardinal's hat", which should contain your position on the map.

This method is most useful in open terrain, for example in hilly country.

Attack point

An attack point is a feature or mapped object, which appears easy to navigate to, and from which it is easier to navigate to your final destination.

Summary

- There are usually several routes between two places.
- The straight route is not always the best alternative.
- You move at different speeds in different types of terrain.
- Line features such as roads, paths and power lines are easy to follow.
- By features we mean distinct and conspicuous features in the terrain such as a lake or a large hill.
- Attack points are easy-to-find features, which are nearest to the location you are navigating to.

5. Extreme navigation

Poor visibility

To get some idea about how difficult it is to navigate in mist, fog and cloud, is to imagine trying to find your way in total darkness or deep in a featureless forest.

If you achieve half the speed of travel that you can reasonably expect on a clear sunny day, you will be doing well. Be prepared to go much slower. A lot more time is spent at night, reading the map and compass. Also, you are likely to go off-route and therefore have to re-locate.

Because you will be moving more slowly and in fact standing still for longer periods, you should wear warm clothing.

In poor visibility you must rely much more on dead reckoning (direction and distance). The reason of course, is that fewer, sometimes very few features can be seen.

Reading the fine detail of a map is a lot more difficult in the dark, especially for anyone whose sight is not near-perfect. Looking at the map in the light of a bright headlamp or torch, creates the loss of night vision. It pays, therefore, to illuminate the map with just enough light to read the map.

High speed

World class elite orienteerers are the fastest navigators on foot. The average orienteerer, who tries to run too fast through complicated terrain, will make many mistakes. The most common cause of mistakes is not taking a long enough look at the map. Good orienteerers take less than two seconds to look at the map and make a route selection and even less to check their position along the route. In complex terrain you should look at the map for twice as long and yet we are only talking about up to four seconds instead of two!

The strange thing about running fast through the forest is that you get a better sense of direction, providing you keep an eye on the features ahead. If you spend too much time looking at the map, you tend not to notice that you have changed your direction of travel.

Very tough terrain

Two things happen. You can be forced a long way off route and distances always seem longer, so you start looking for the location too early, moving off left or right when you should keep going straight ahead.

Featureless terrain

With no features around (it is rather like navigating at sea) there is nothing to guide you. It may not be tough, but navigation may be very difficult.

It is in such terrain, that a GPS instrument comes into its own.

In addition to the biggest benefit of being able to fix your position, the GPS instrument is able to tell you accurately how far you have travelled. A position "fix" does this, of course, but measuring distance travelled has always been a big problem to the navigator on foot.

Your equipment

Exploration is fun and navigation can add to the fun, providing you use the correct equipment and the equipment is in good condition.

Should you become lost and as a result get cold, tired and injured, don't be too quick to blame your equipment. There are a few questions you have to ask yourself first, because good quality products rarely fail. Ask yourself:

• **Was the equipment really in perfect condition when you left base?**
• **Did you select the right equipment and spares for the expedition in question?**
A good example is bulbs, often essential, but they often fail.
• **Did you use and care for the equipment correctly?**
• **Did you rely too much on your equipment and not enough on your skills and experience as an explorer?**

Finally, far too often equipment is blamed when in fact lack of physical fitness may have been the root cause of the problem!

If you plan to walk for 8 hours, but through making mistakes (at the planning stage or during the walk) finish up 12 or even 16 hours, will you be fit enough to cope? Mistakes are usually due to poor navigation.

A common mistake when navigating in extreme conditions is guessing. Being tired, trying to keep to an important expected time of arrival (ETA) and maybe finding yourself in a potentially dangerous situation, make it very tempting to guess the way forward rather than to trust your instruments and what you see on the map. It is very easy to make the map fit the ground, or vice versa, when you are lost and desperate!

SILVA ECLIPSE PRO 99
– an extreme navigation compass

The ECLIPSE PRO 99 is a unique compass with various navigation features. It's needleless design, using a patented alignment system, makes it accurate to 0.5 degree. It also features survival/information cards describing basic survival technique, navigation tips, first aid info, Romer scales and engineers functions such as vertical angle measurement and different conversion scales.

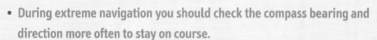

- During extreme navigation you should check the compass bearing and direction more often to stay on course.
- It pays to study the map and to find a route that stays on the same altitude in order to avoid a lot of climbing.
- Get into a routine of checking the condition of your equipment and your skills in using it before going out in the wilderness.

6. Testing
and practising

Theoretical knowledge (map reading) is not enough. Theory needs to be combined with practical training (navigation). This chapter gives examples of possible training sessions ranging from the simple and secure to more adventurous alternatives.

As we noted in the introductory chapter, the amount of detail and the standard of maps vary. For example, on a map at a scale of 1:10 000 far more features and objects are marked than on a map at 1:50 000. Maps to the same scale can differ in quality. The best and most detailed maps are those that have been specially drawn for the sport of orienteering.

Map walk – stage 1

Use a map showing a lit track or a marked hiking track. Follow the track at the same time as you follow the map. Remember to keep the map oriented at all times. Your compass will help you.

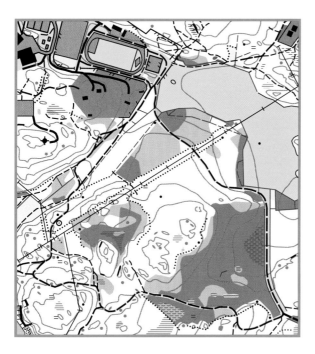

• Note all the objects and features that you pass. See how they are indicated on the map with different symbols and colours.

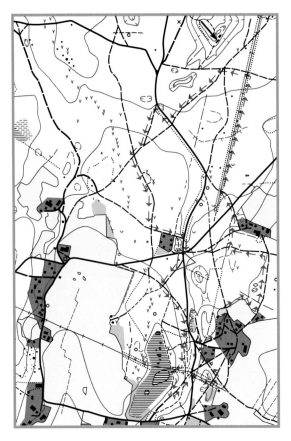

Map walk – stage 2

This practice starts in the same way as stage 1, but you then depart from the marked track or path. Use different line features that link up.

• In this example you follow the road for a bit and then the power line, etc. You can draw your route on the map before starting.

Peak survey

Find a high place. Go to the top and look around you. Note where the terrain is steep or where it slopes gently and study how this is shown on

the map. Visit a hollow, a re-entrant, a spur or a valley and study how it is shown on the map.

• Lift your gaze a little and try to identify buildings or other prominent objects. Where are they on the map?

Short cuts

The idea is that you should now stop following line features and make your way across terrain without line features. The compass will show you the direction to travel in. Move towards prominent line features that cannot be missed as in the example on the right.

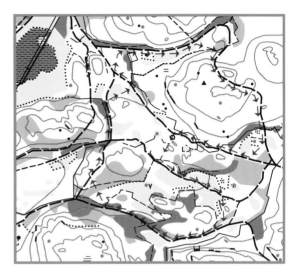

Compass star

Practise taking compass bearings and following them. Start from a fixed point on the map and mark 5 or 6 objects at a distance. These should be prominent objects which are difficult to miss, for example a road junction or the edge of a field.

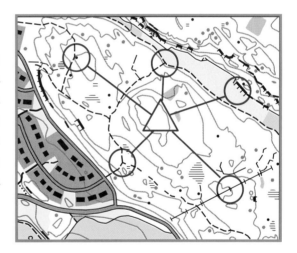

• Take a bearing to one of the objects and go to it. Return to your starting point and then take a bearing to the next object.

75

Selecting a route

Mark a starting point and three or four objects that you intend to pass. Select two different routes to the respective objects.

• Visit each of the objects following one of your routes. Back again at the starting point visit the objects again using the other route.

Follow your neighbour

This practice involves from two to four participants. One of them has the map and chooses a object and moves to it. The others follow and try to memorise prominent and conspicuous features that they pass.

When they arrive at the destination, those who have been following have to point out on the map where they are and how they got there. After that, another member of the group chooses a new destination and leads the way to it.

7. Let's go!

When you have learnt how to use a map and compass, you can use your skills in many different ways. You can find new terrain and new routes for your walks. You will be better able to locate and relocate places and keep to your intended route. You will be able to find your way among the maze of streets and alleys in the city.

Orienteering – an exciting alternative

The sport of orienteering was born at the end of the nineteenth century. The idea is to use a map and compass to find a number of features. Competitive orienteering involves visiting the features, known as controls, as fast as possible. The winner is the person who has visited all the controls in the fastest time. A typical orienteering course is shown on the map below.

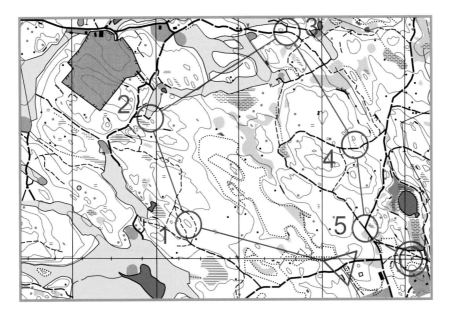

The start is marked with a triangle. The exact starting point is at the centre of the triangle. The controls that you are to visit, are shown as circles and the finish is the one marked with a double ring. The controls are linked, by straight lines but this does not mean that you have to go "straight there". You choose your route yourself. But you have to visit the controls in the right order, 1, 2, 3, etc.

Each control is marked with an orange and white orienteering marker. At the marker there is a stamping device (orienteering punch) for marking the control card you are given at the start. This is your "proof" that you have visited the control.

The stamping device either makes holes mechanically as the picture in the middle or is an electronic recording device (shown right).

Orienteering marker
Orienteering marker 30 × 30 cm, IOF-std. is orange/white and shows the control position in the terrain.

Orienteering punches

Electronic punching system (EMIT®)

TEST YOURSELF

The map on the previous page shows an orienteering course with 5 controls. State the following points for each leg:
• How would you get from the starting point to each respective control?
• Which features in the terrain would you look out for and pass on your way to the respective controls?

The course that you have just been dealing with is an example of a novice course as used for competition. For more advanced competitors the courses are more difficult. Below is an advanced course. The only things that it has in common with the novice course are the start and finish.

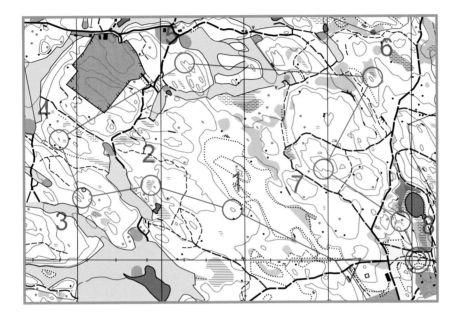

The map above shows an orienteering course with 8 controls. State the following points for each leg:
• Which possible routes are there for each leg?
• Which is the "best" route?
• Which features in the terrain would you specially look out for and pass on your way to each control?

Competition for everyone

In competitions there are classes suited to most categories of orienteerers. Classes take into consideration sex, age and skill at orienteering. Normally there are a lot of classes at an event.

Your national sports council should be able to put you in touch with the national orienteering federation.

TRIM-orienteering

TRIM-orienteering is a popular form of non-competitive orienteering. From 30–50 controls are placed in the terrain for a longer period of time. (A week or longer)

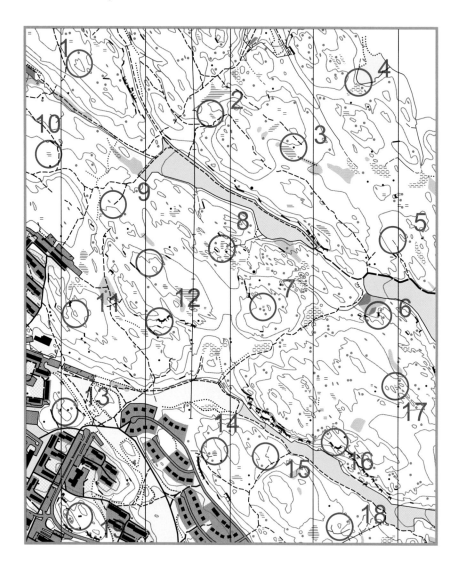

All the controls are shown on the map. You look for all or some of them without a time limit as and when you have the opportunity. The controls are orange and white. You mark your control card at these controls.

MTB orienteering

This is arranged in the same way as normal foot-orienteering with the difference that you use a bicycle to get to the controls. The routes keep mainly to roads and paths.

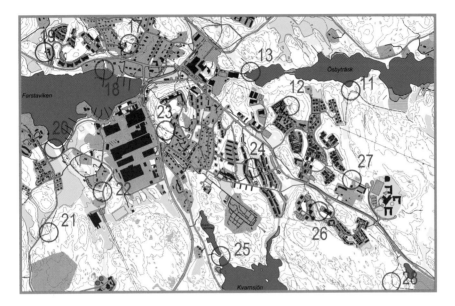

Permanent courses

Many parks have permanent courses set up. They usually consist of "feature" posts set in the ground at sites, or small 10 cm square markers positioned on trees, which vary from easy to difficult to find

A map pack is available from the park warden, the park centre kiosk, the local orienteering club or even the local library. In the pack you should find a map which may be pre-marked. If it is not, there will be a master map near the start, from which you can copy the controls you wish to visit.

In addition to the map, you may be given some advice and various courses, of varying difficulty.

These courses make perfect training areas and provide a very good way for the complete novice to be introduced to the sport of orienteering.

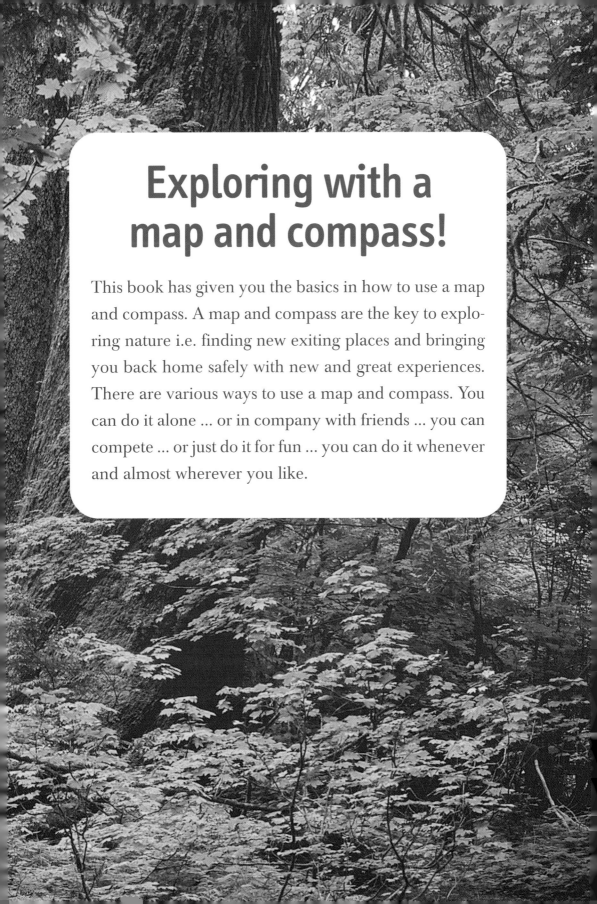

Exploring with a map and compass!

This book has given you the basics in how to use a map and compass. A map and compass are the key to exploring nature i.e. finding new exiting places and bringing you back home safely with new and great experiences. There are various ways to use a map and compass. You can do it alone ... or in company with friends ... you can compete ... or just do it for fun ... you can do it whenever and almost wherever you like.

Answers

Page 10

A = 5 metres

B = 50 metres

C = 200 metres

D = 15 metres

E = 2 000 metres

Page 14–15

A = 7	E = 10	I = 11
B = 9	F = 2	J = 3
C = 4	G = 8	K = 12
D = 5	H = 1	L = 6

Page 16

1 = Lake/open water

2 = Cliff/rock face

3 = Fence corner

4 = Watercourse

5 = Building

6 = Road

7 = Vehicle track

8 = Boulder

9 = Open land, clearing

10 = Small path

11 = Waterhole

12 = Marsh

13 = Road (asphalt)

14 = Knoll

15 = Built up area

A = 220 metres

B = 330 metres

C = 450 metres

D = 380 metres

E = 580 metres

Page 20

• Boulder, small tower, ruin, cairn, boulder field.

• There are eight peaks numbered 1 to 8.

• Peaks on the same altitude are:

– 1 and 2

– 3, 4 and 5

– 6 and 7

• the arrows indicate steep slopes.

• "X" indicates the deepest depression

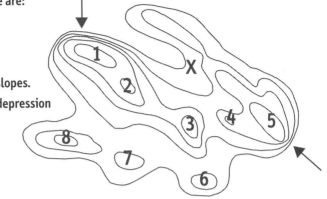

1 = Uphill

2 = Downhill

3 = Flat

4 = Downhill

5 = Uphill

Page 21

1 = C	5 = H
2 = B	6 = A
3 = F	7 = G
4 = E	8 = D

Page 22–23

A = 3	F = 5
B = 4	G = 7
C = 8	H = 9
D = 1	I = 2
E = 6	J = 10

Page 24

1 = Flat	6 = Flat
2 = Uphill	7 = Flat
3 = Flat	8 = Uphill
4 = Flat	9 = Uphill
5 = Downhill	10 = Downhill

Page 25

1	= Re-entrant	6	= Ridge
2	= Ridge	7	= Re-entrant
3	= Re-entrant	8	= Re-entrant
4	= Re-entrant	9	= Re-entrant
5	= Ridge	10	= Ridge

Page 27

1 = B
2 = C
3 = A

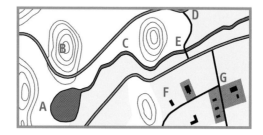

Page 38

1 = C   2 = D   3 = A   4 = B

Page 42 +/- 3° is accepted

1	= 34°	6	= 243°
2	= 80°	7	= 270°
3	= 140°	8	= 300°
4	= 158°	9	= 329°
5	= 202°	10	= 356°

Page 58

- Line features/Handrail are indicated on the map.
- Easiest to follow are paths, power-lines and fences.

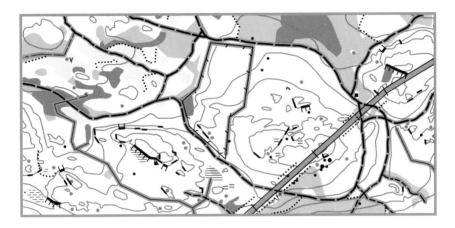

- Main features are marked on the map.

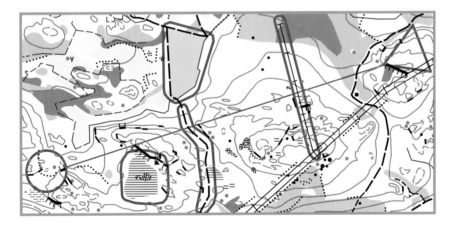

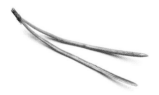

Page 60

• Route-choices – two examples.

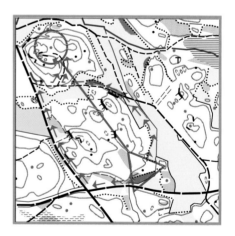

Make a peak!

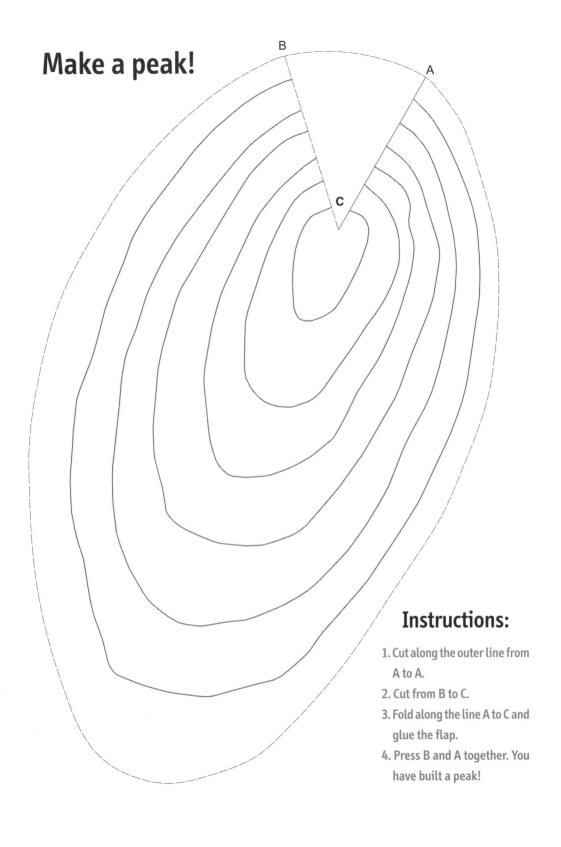

Instructions:

1. Cut along the outer line from A to A.
2. Cut from B to C.
3. Fold along the line A to C and glue the flap.
4. Press B and A together. You have built a peak!

Notes

Notes

Notes

Notes